# Oxford Read and Discover

## 4 Discover!

# Why We Recycle

Fiona Undrill

**OXFORD**

UNIVERSITY PRESS

# OXFORD
UNIVERSITY PRESS

Great Clarendon Street, Oxford OX2 6DP

Oxford University Press is a department of the University of Oxford. It furthers the University's objective of excellence in research, scholarship, and education by publishing worldwide in

Oxford New York

Auckland Cape Town Dar es Salaam Hong Kong Karachi Kuala Lumpur Madrid Melbourne Mexico City Nairobi New Delhi Shanghai Taipei Toronto

With offices in

Argentina Austria Brazil Chile Czech Republic France Greece Guatemala Hungary Italy Japan Poland Portugal Singapore South Korea Switzerland Thailand Turkey Ukraine Vietnam

OXFORD and OXFORD ENGLISH are registered trade marks of Oxford University Press in the UK and in certain other countries

© Oxford University Press 2011

The moral rights of the author have been asserted

Database right Oxford University Press (maker)

First published 2011

2021
24

Any websites referred to in this publication are in the public domain and their addresses are provided by Oxford University Press for information only. Oxford University Press disclaims any responsibility for the content

ISBN: 978 0 19 464444 0

An Audio Pack containing this book and an Audio download is also available, ISBN 978 0 19 402210 1

This book is also available as an e-Book, ISBN 978 0 19 464730 4

An accompanying Activity Book is also available, ISBN 978 0 19 464454 9

Printed in China

This book is printed on paper from certified and well-managed sources.

ACKNOWLEDGEMENTS

*Illustrations by*: Arlene Adams p.11, 30; Kelly Kennedy pp.5, 6, 13, 18; Dusan Pavlic/Beehive Illustration pp.34, 46, 47; Alan Rowe pp.24, 28, 32, 34, 46, 47; Mark Ruffle p.9.

*The Publishers would also like to thank the following for their kind permission to reproduce photographs and other copyright material*: Alamy pp.5 (apple/Chris Edgcombe), 8 (cars/dpa picture alliance archive), 10 (Yilar Hendia), 12 (Avalon/Construction Photography), 13 (fleece/Angela Hampton Picture Library) 15 (Birger Lallo/Nordicphotos), 19 (Bildagentur-online), 23 (Dmytro Zinkevych); Getty Images pp.3 (plastic waste/ Randy Faris/The Image Bank), 8 (plastic waste/Randy Faris/ The Image Bank), 9 (Rebecca Emery/Riser/paper, clothes/ Vuk8691/iStock); Magna Glaskeramik GmbH/Low Impact Ltd p.14 (Structuran Jade hammered type rain screen Museum facade in Germany); Oxford University Press pp.3 (food waste/glass/Alamy, metal/Corel, paper/Digital Vision/Getty, recycling bins/Photodisc/Getty), 4 (Stockbyte/ Getty), 8 (glass/Alamy, cans), 9 (cans/Corbis), 16 (metal for recycling/Shutterstock), 18 (Alamy), 20 (chimneys); Mark Ruffle p.7; Shutterstock p.13 (plastic pellets/Suteelak phundang), 16 (aluminium in rock/Showcake), 17 (Razvy), 20 (swan/Izzy-Belle), 22 (Photographee.eu).

# Introduction

We all make a lot of waste. There's waste from our homes, factories, offices, and schools. We recycle a lot of our waste materials, but we should recycle more. Do you know why?

food

plastic

metal

paper

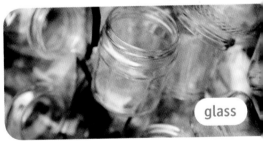
glass

What do you throw away?
What is your waste made of?
What waste materials do you recycle?

Discover!

Now read and discover more about why we recycle waste!

# Too Much Waste

In some countries, one person can make about 5 kilograms of waste every day! Where does all this waste go? Most waste goes to a landfill. At a landfill, people put the waste under the ground. Landfills are very big because we make so much waste.

**A Landfill**

Most waste materials decompose – they break down into very small pieces. Food waste decomposes fast, but some waste materials decompose slowly. Paper materials take from two to five months to decompose, some metal materials take from 80 to 100 years, and plastic materials take maybe up to 1,000 years. Some materials, like glass, never decompose.

We are making more and more waste. We need more landfills, but there's no more land on Earth for landfills. Our waste stays in landfills for too long, and this is bad for Earth. So we should make less waste – we should recycle more things.

**Discover!**

Around the world, people make up to 4 billion metric tons of waste every year.

Go to pages 24–25 for activities.

5

# Reduce, Reuse, Recycle

Fixing a Skateboard

We should put less waste in landfills. We can help to do this when we reduce, reuse, and recycle our waste. When we reduce our waste, we make less waste. We can help to do this when we only buy things that we really need. We can also borrow things, or fix things when they break. When we don't buy so many things, we reduce waste.

When we reuse something, we use it again. When we buy a bottle of water, we can put more water in the bottle when we finish it – we don't need to buy a new bottle.

**Discover!**

We should reuse our plastic bags. Around the world, people use about one million plastic bags every day – we usually use one bag for only about 12 minutes!

When we recycle something, we use it to make something new. We can recycle most glass, paper, and metal. We can recycle some plastic.

We can recycle things to make more of the same thing, for example, we can recycle paper to make new paper. We can also make something different, like this radio that's made of recycled metal.

**A Radio Made of Recycled Metal**

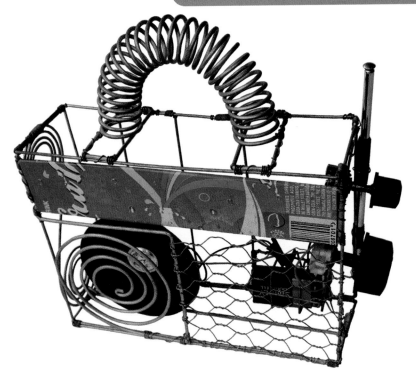

→ Go to pages 26–27 for activities.

# What Can We Recycle?

bottles

jars

cars

We can recycle most things – clothes, shoes, phones, computers, televisions, cars, cans, paper, bottles, and batteries. There are a few things that we can't recycle – but not many!

We can recycle most paper and card to make new paper. We can recycle metal from many different things, like cans, cars, and computers. It's hard to get new metal, so it's good to recycle old metal.

We can recycle most types of glass. It's good to sort the glass into different colors – green, brown, and clear glass. Factories can only make new clear glass when 99% of the recycled glass is clear.

cans

clothes

paper

There's a recycling symbol on a lot of the things that we can recycle. There's sometimes a symbol on the things that we can't recycle.

We have to recycle different types of plastic in different ways. The recycling symbols on plastic help people to sort the different types of plastic.

## Recycling Symbols

can recycle

can't recycle

can recycle this type of plastic

→ Go to pages 28–29 for activities.

# 4 Paper

Paper is made from trees, so when we recycle used paper to make new paper, we save trees. Our used paper goes to a paper recycling factory. Here, machines cut the paper and put the pieces in water. This makes the paper into fibers. Then, machines wash the fibers to take out things like staples and glue.

Next, machines put in soap and they blow air through the water and fibers. This makes bubbles. Ink stays on the bubbles, and machines take out the inky bubbles to make the fibers clean. Then machines use the fibers to make new paper.

**Making New Paper**

Every time we recycle paper, the fibers get smaller and weaker, and then they are not so good for making new paper. This means that we can only recycle paper from four to six times. So we will always need some new trees to make paper.

Recycling a Newspaper

newspaper factory

paper recycling factory

**Discover!**

In seven days, we can get a new newspaper from a recycled newspaper!

Go to pages 30–31 for activities.

# 5 Plastic

Plastic For Sorting

Plastic is newer than a lot of other materials. No one really knows how long it takes to decompose – maybe up to 1,000 years. Around the world, people make more than 200 million metric tons of plastic every year. All this plastic is probably still on Earth!

We don't recycle much plastic because it's hard to sort the different types of plastic, and there aren't many factories that recycle plastic. We can recycle plastic from bottles, and from parts of refrigerators and cars.

People sort the different types of plastic, and then they take them to a plastic recycling factory.

Different factories recycle different types of plastic. At the factory, machines clean the plastic and cut it into small pieces. Other machines melt the plastic and clean it

**Recycled Plastic Pellets**

again. Then, machines cut this clean plastic into small pellets. Other factories use these pellets to make new plastic things.

We can use recycled plastic to make phones, clothes, chairs, toys – and much more!

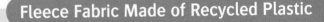

**Fleece Fabric Made of Recycled Plastic**

**Discover!**

About 25 big plastic bottles can make one fleece jacket!

➜ Go to pages 32–33 for activities. 13

# 6 Glass

Glass is one of the best materials for recycling because we can recycle it again and again. We use most recycled glass to make new glass things, like glass bottles. Sometimes, we can see it in buildings because we can use recycled glass to make walls and windows.

## Recycled Glass on Walls

The Greenhouse Effect Ltd

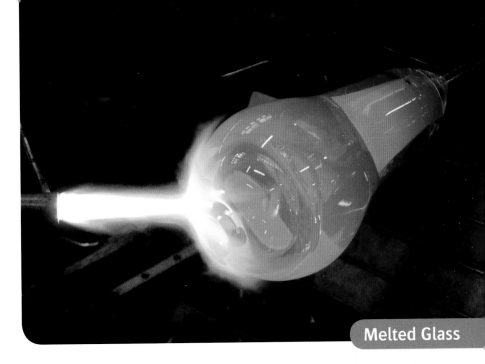

Glass is made from sand. To make glass, people make sand very, very hot so that it melts. Recycled glass doesn't have to get so hot to melt. So it's good to make new glass from recycled glass, because we save energy.

At a glass recycling factory, people sort the glass into different colors. Then, machines break the glass into small pieces. Other machines clean the glass – magnets take out any metal, and air blows off any plastic and paper. Then the glass is made into much smaller pieces. Other factories melt the very small pieces of glass to make new glass things.

→ Go to pages 34–35 for activities.

# 7 Metal

**Metal for Recycling**

There are lots of different metals and they all come from rocks. To get most metals out of rocks, people have to use machines to make the rocks very, very hot. The machines use a lot of energy. It's good to recycle metals because we save this energy. Metal is a good material to recycle because we can recycle it again and again.

**Aluminum in Rock**

We can recycle all metals, but we recycle different metals in different ways. Let's look at aluminum.

Aluminum is the metal in most drinks cans. It's also in planes, cars, bicycles, computers, buildings, and things that we cook with!

At the recycling factory, machines cut the waste aluminum into small pieces. Then, very hot air blows off all the words and pictures on the metal. Next, machines melt the metal and make bars. Other factories melt these bars to make new metal things.

**Aluminum Bars**

Discover!

Aluminum bars are very, very big – one bar can make more than one million drinks cans.

Go to pages 36–37 for activities.

**8 Food Waste**

banana skin

egg shell

What do you do with the food that you don't eat? In some countries, people throw away billions of metric tons of food waste every year. Some of it is food that we can't eat, like banana skins and egg shells, but some of it is good food. Most of it goes to landfills. In landfills there's no air under the ground, so food decomposes very slowly.

We can make compost with some of our food waste. We can do this at home – the compost helps plants to grow in the garden.

**Discover!**

In a compost bin, worms eat the waste and make it into compost.

A Biodigester

In many places, people collect food waste from homes, stores, and restaurants. Machines called biodigesters use the food waste to make compost for farms. When the food decomposes, it makes a gas. People can use this gas to cook with, or to make electricity.

We can reduce waste and save money when we only buy food that we need. We should think carefully about what food we need to buy, so that we don't waste it.

→ Go to pages 38–39 for activities.

# 9 Problems for Earth

Pollution makes land, air, and water dirty. Factories make pollution, and landfills make pollution, too. Polluted air and water can make people and animals sick.

People throw some waste onto the ground or into rivers. This waste makes more pollution and more problems. Polluted rivers can kill the plants and animals that live there.

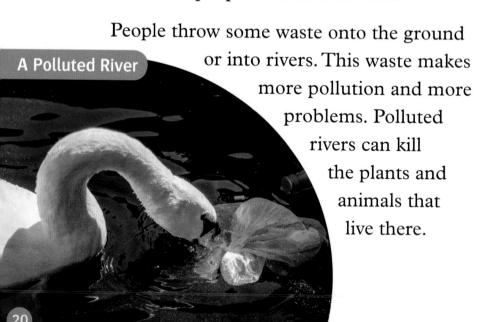

**A Polluted River**

All around the world, people make lots of new things every day. We need materials like paper and plastic to make these things. Paper is made from trees. Plastic is usually made from oil. Many factories use oil for the energy that they need to make machines work, or to make things very hot. Earth gives us trees and oil. We need to use them carefully, so that we can have them in the future.

We are making too many new things, and using too many materials. We are also making too much waste. We can't live like this forever. We are making too many problems for Earth.

→ Go to pages 40–41 for activities.

 # What Can You Do?

You can do a lot of things – every little thing helps! You can reduce your waste. Don't buy too many new things. Do you really need a new computer game? Can you borrow one from a friend? Fix things when they break.

You can reuse and recycle your waste. Make things from waste! Look at your waste and see what you can do with it. On the Internet, you can find lots of great ideas, for example, how to make games, clothes, and bags.

**Lanterns Made From Waste**

**Picking Up Waste for Recycling**

Recycling can be easy! At home, you can use recycling boxes. Or maybe you can use different wastebaskets for different types of waste. At school, you can recycle lots of things, too. When you are outside, you can pick up waste for recycling, but be careful – don't pick up dangerous waste.

Remember! We should all reduce, reuse, and recycle our waste!

→ Go to pages 42–43 for activities.

# 1 Too Much Waste

← Read pages 4–5.

## 1 Circle the correct words.

1 In some **countries** / **landfills**, one person can make about **five** / **fifteen** kilograms of waste every **year** / **day**.

2 Landfills are very **big** / **small**.

3 Food waste decomposes **slowly** / **fast**.

4 Metal materials decompose **slowly** / **fast**.

5 Glass materials **always** / **never** decompose.

6 We should make **more** / **less** waste.

## 2 Match.

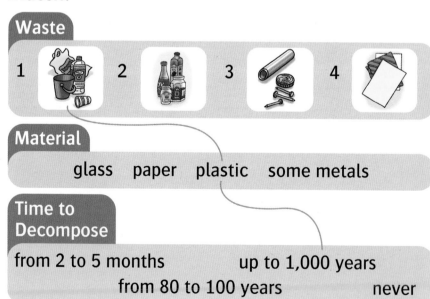

**Waste**

1    2    3    4

**Material**

glass   paper   plastic   some metals

**Time to Decompose**

from 2 to 5 months    up to 1,000 years

from 80 to 100 years    never

## 3 Complete the sentences.

> waste   never   less   ~~landfill~~
> months   5 kilograms   years   waste

1 Most waste goes to a ___landfill___ .

2 Landfills are very big because we make so much _____ .

3 One person can make about _____ of waste every day.

4 Food _____ decomposes fast.

5 Some materials _____ decompose.

6 Paper materials take from two to five _____ to decompose.

7 Some metal materials take from 80 to 100 _____ to decompose.

8 We should make _____ waste.

## 4 What waste do you throw away?

_____

_____

_____

_____

_____

# 2 Reduce, Reuse, Recycle

← Read pages 6–7.

## 1 Match. Then write the sentences.

When we reduce our waste,
When we reuse our waste,
When we recycle our waste,
We should
We can fix things

we use it again.
we use it to make
something new.
put less waste
in landfills.
when they break.
we make less waste.

1  When we reduce our waste, we make less waste.

2  _____

3  _____

4  _____

5  _____

## 2 Write *true* or *false*.

1  People should put more waste in landfills.     false

2  It's good to fix things when they break.        _____

3  We can recycle most glass, paper,
   and metal.                                       _____

4  We usually use one plastic bag for
   about a week.                                    _____

## 3 Complete the sentences.

use   reduce   reuse   recycle

1 We should reduce, _____ , and recycle
   our waste.

2 When we make less waste, we _____
   our waste.

3 When we _____ things, we use them to
   make something new.

4 Around the world, people _____ one million
   plastic bags every day.

## 4 Find and write the words. Then write the odd one out.

recyclereusereducewastelandfill
elephantglassmetalplasticpaper

1 __recycle__    5 _____    9 _____

2 _____    6 _____    10 _____

3 _____    7 _____

4 _____    8 _____

The odd one out is: _____

## 5 Write ✓ or ✗.

At home, we recycle things made of:

paper ☐    glass ☐    plastic ☐    metal ☐

# 3 What Can We Recycle?

← Read pages 8–9.

## 1 Write the words.

> clothes ~~batteries~~ computer
> television cans shoes

 1 <u>batteries</u>

 4 _____

 2 _____

 5 _____

 3 _____

 6 _____

## 2 Circle the correct words.

1 There's a recycling symbol on a lot of the things that we can **recycle** / **reuse**.

2 Factories can only make new clear glass when 99% of the recycled glass is **green** / **clear**.

3 We can recycle metal from **many** / **some** different things.

4 Recycling **symbols** / **landfills** help people to sort the different types of plastic.

**3** **Complete the sentences.**

colors   glass   recycle   good   plastic   cars   new

1  There's a recycling symbol on a lot of the things that we can _____ .

2  We can recycle most paper and card to make _____ paper.

3  We can recycle most types of _____ .

4  When we recycle glass, it's good to sort it into different _____ .

5  We have to recycle different types of _____ in different ways.

6  It's _____ to recycle old metal.

7  We can recycle metal from cans, _____ , and computers.

**4** **Answer the questions.**

1  What is on a lot of the things that we can recycle?
   There's a recycling symbol.

2  What metal things can we recycle?

   _____

3  Can we recycle everything?

   _____

# 4 Paper

← Read pages 10–11.

paper recycling factory
newspaper factory
newspaper

**1 Write the words.**

1 _____

2 _____

3 _____

**2 Find and write the words.**

paperfactorymachinesfibersinkgluestaplestreessoapair

1 _____   5 _____   9 _____

2 _____   6 _____   10 _____

3 _____   7 _____

4 _____   8 _____

**3 Write *true* or *false*.**

1 Paper is made from sand. _____

2 When we recycle paper, we save trees. _____

3 We can get a new newspaper from
a recycled newspaper in a week. _____

4 We can only recycle paper three times. _____

## 4 Write correct sentences.

1 Paper is made from cars.

   <u>Paper is made from trees.</u>

2 When we recycle chocolate, we save trees.

   _____

3 At a paper recycling factory, machines cut
   the paper and put the pieces in pizzas.

   _____

4 Machines wash paper fibers to take out things
   like dogs and cats.

   _____

5 Every time we recycle paper, the fibers get bigger
   and stronger.

   _____

6 We will always need some new bottles to make
   paper.

   _____

## 5 Write ✓ or ✗.

Waste paper in my home comes from:

newspapers ☐    mail ☐

birthday cards ☐    drawing paper ☐

comic books ☐    writing paper ☐

# 5 Plastic

← Read pages 12–13.

## 1 Write the words.

bottle   phone   car
toys   refrigerator   chair

 1 _____

 4 _____

 2 _____

 5 _____

 3 _____

 6 _____

## 2 Complete the sentences.

bottles   decompose   factory   different   clothes

1 No one really knows how long plastic takes
to _____ .

2 It's hard to sort the _____ types of plastic.

3 We can recycle plastic from things like _____ .

4 We can use recycled plastic to make things like
_____ , phones, chairs, and toys.

5 At a plastic recycling _____ , machines clean
the plastic and cut it into small pieces.

**3 Order the words.**

1 materials. / other / newer than / Plastic is

   Plastic is newer than other materials.

2 that recycle plastic. / many factories / There aren't

   _____

3 things like / bottles. / We can recycle / plastic from

   _____

4 different types / of plastic. / Different factories / recycle

   _____

5 clothes. / We can use / recycled plastic / to make

   _____

**4 Number the sentences in order.**

**How Machines Recycle Plastic:**

[ ] They clean the plastic again.

[ ] They cut the plastic into small pieces.

[1] They clean the plastic.

[ ] They melt the plastic.

[ ] They cut the clean plastic into pellets.

# 6 Glass

← Read pages 14–15.

## 1 Write the words.

machine   hot   melt   magnet   blow   sand

1 _____

4 _____

2 _____

5 _____

3 _____

6 _____

## 2 Match.

1  Glass is
2  People sort the glass
3  Machines break the glass
4  When we make new glass from recycled glass
5  People can recycle
6  We use most recycled glass to

glass again and again.

made from sand.

make new glass things.

into small pieces.

we can save energy.

into different colors.

**3** **Write _true_ or _false_.**

1 To make glass, people make trees very,
   very hot. _____

2 Recycled glass doesn't have to get so
   hot to melt. _____

3 At a glass recycling factory, magnets take
   out any metal. _____

4 At a glass recycling factory, water blows
   off any plastic and paper. _____

5 It's good to recycle glass. _____

6 We can only recycle glass three times. _____

**4** **Complete the sentences.**

> energy   sand   pieces
> recycled   factory   materials

1 Glass is made from _____.

2 When we make new glass from recycled glass, we
   save _____.

3 Glass is one of the best _____ for recycling.

4 We use most _____ glass to make new
   glass things.

5 At a glass recycling _____, machines break
   the glass into small _____.

# 7 Metal

## 1 Find and write the words.

| m | a | l | u | m | i | n | u | m | e |
|---|---|---|---|---|---|---|---|---|---|
| e | a | o | b | a | r | s | o | h | n |
| t | t | o | n | p | u | s | e | r | e |
| a | h | r | r | o | c | k | s | n | r |
| l | o | n | o | n | b | l | u | p | g |
| s | t | p | l | o | n | e | e | n | y |

1 It's good to recycle _____metals_____.

2 One type of metal is called _____.

3 When we recycle metals, we save _____.

4 Metals come from _____.

5 When something isn't cold it's _____.

6 One aluminum _____ makes lots of cans.

## 2 Complete the sentences.

energy   different   rocks   recycle

1 There are lots of _____ metals.

2 Metals come from _____.

3 We save _____ when we recycle metal.

4 We can _____ metal again and again.

## 3 Order the words.

1 energy / metals. / We save / when we / recycle

_____

2 different metals / We recycle / different ways. / in

_____

3 is the metal / drinks cans. / Aluminum / in / most

_____

4 metals. / can / recycle / all / We

_____

5 are / Aluminum / big. / very / bars

_____

## 4 Answer the questions.

1 Where do metals come from?

_____

2 Why is metal a good material to recycle?

_____

3 What type of metal are most drinks cans made from?

_____

4 How do machines make aluminum bars?

_____

5 How many drinks cans can one aluminum bar make?

_____

# 8 Food Waste

← Read pages 18–19.

## 1 Match. Then write the sentences.

We can't eat
In landfills
We can reduce waste
We can make compost
Compost helps

plants to grow.
with our food waste.
food decomposes
very slowly.
banana skins.
when we only buy the
food that we need.

1 _____

2 _____

3 _____

4 _____

5 _____

## 2 Complete the chart.

| | Breakfast | Lunch | Dinner |
|---|---|---|---|
| My Food Waste Today | | | |

**3 Write true or false.**

1 In some countries, people throw away
billions of metric tons of banana skins. _____

2 In landfills, there's no waste so food
decomposes very slowly. _____

3 When we only buy food that we are going
to eat, we reduce waste and save money. _____

4 We can make compost with some of
our food waste. _____

5 In many places, people collect food
waste from homes, stores, and restaurants. _____

6 When food decomposes, it makes a gas
that people can use to make electricity. _____

**4 Complete the puzzle. Then find the secret word.**

1 What we eat.
2 We can't eat the skin of this fruit.
3 Compost helps plants to grow here.
4 In landfills, food does this slowly.
5 We can make this with our food waste.

```
1 →  f  o  o  d
2 →
3 →
4 →
5 →
```

The secret word is: ☐☐☐☐☐

# 9 Problems for Earth

Read pages 20–21.

**1 Match. Then write the sentences.**

Glass is made from          oil.
Paper is made from          rocks.
Plastic is made from        sand.
Metal comes from            trees.

1 _____

2 _____

3 _____

4 _____

**2 Find and write the words. Then write the odd one out.**

oiltreesyellowproblemspollutionfactoriesenergywaste

1 _____      5 _____

2 _____      6 _____

3 _____      7 _____

4 _____      8 _____

The odd one out is: _____

40

## 3 Circle the odd one out.

1  oil  (plastic)  trees  plants

2  dirty  polluted  sick  future

3  waste  air  land  water

4  machines  factories  animals  landfills

## 4 Circle the correct words.

1  **Plants** / **Landfills** make pollution.

2  Pollution **is** / **isn't** a problem for Earth.

3  Polluted rivers can **kill** / **sick** plants and animals.

4  We need to use trees and oil carefully, so that we **can** / **can't** have them in the future.

5  Many factories use oil for the energy that makes **machines** / **people** work.

6  We are making too many **old** / **new** things.

## 5 Answer the questions.

1  What can make pollution?

_____

2  Why are polluted rivers a problem?

_____

3  Why do we need to use trees and oil carefully?

_____

# 10 What Can You Do?

← Read pages 22–23.

**1 Complete the chart.**

cars   glass bottles
plastic bottles   cars   cans
newspapers   birthday cards
computers   plastic boxes

| Things that you can recycle ... | | | |
|---|---|---|---|
| for plastic: | for paper: | for glass: | for metal: |
| cars | | | |
| | | | |
| | | | |

**2 Write correct sentences.**

1 You can reduce your schools.

_____

2 Borrow a computer game from a cat.

_____

3 Fix things when they sing.

_____

4 Write things from waste.

_____

**3** Write *reduce, reuse,* or *recycle.*

1 Fix things when they break.  <u>reduce</u>

2 Make things from waste.  _____

3 Use a water bottle again.  _____

4 Don't buy too many new things.  _____

5 Make compost for the garden.  _____

**4** Write the words.

1 <u>reduce</u>   2 _____   3 _____   4 _____

5 _____   6 _____   7 _____   8 _____

**5** Complete the sentences.

1 To reduce the waste that I make, I can _____
_____

2 To reuse more things, I can _____
_____

3 To recycle more things, I can _____
_____

# A Recycling Poster

**1** **Think about recycling. Write notes.**

Write eight things that we can recycle.

_____   _____   _____   _____

_____   _____   _____   _____

Write six things that we can make from recycled materials.

_____   _____   _____

_____   _____   _____

Why do we recycle waste?

_Recycling is a good idea because_ _____

_____

_____

_____

**2** **Make a poster. Write about recycling and add pictures.**

**3** **Display your poster.**

# A Recycling Survey

**1** Interview your friends and family.
Write ✓ or ✗.

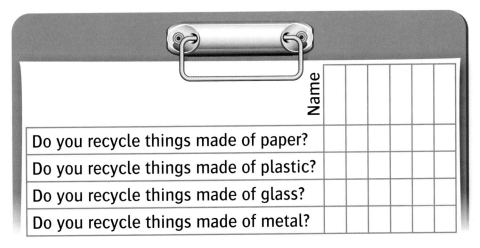

| | Name | | | | |
|---|---|---|---|---|---|
| Do you recycle things made of paper? | | | | | |
| Do you recycle things made of plastic? | | | | | |
| Do you recycle things made of glass? | | | | | |
| Do you recycle things made of metal? | | | | | |

**2** What do people recycle? Count the answers and draw a graph.

| 6 | | | | |
|---|---|---|---|---|
| 5 | | | | |
| 4 | | | | |
| 3 | | | | |
| 2 | | | | |
| 1 | | | | |
| | paper | plastic | glass | metal |

**3** Copy the graph and write about your survey.

**4** Display your survey.

# Picture Dictionary

 batteries

 billion

 blow

 bubbles

 cans

 clothes

 cut

 dangerous waste

 dirty

 Earth

 electricity

 factory

 fibers

 food

 gas

 glass

 ground

 grow

 ink

 kill

 machine

 magnet

 melt

 metal

 million

 newspaper

 oil

 paper

 plastic

 pollution

 recycle

 refrigerator

 river

 rocks

 sand

 soap

 sort

 staple

 throw away

 waste

# Oxford Read and Discover

Series Editor: Hazel Geatches • CLIL Adviser: John Clegg

**Oxford Read and Discover** graded readers are at six levels, for students from age 6 and older. They cover many topics within three subject areas, and support English across the curriculum, or Content and Language Integrated Learning (CLIL).

Available for each reader:
- Audio Pack
- Activity Book

Available for selected readers:
- e-Books

Teaching notes & CLIL guidance: **www.oup.com/elt/teacher/readanddiscover**

| Subject Area / Level | The World of Science & Technology | The Natural World | The World of Arts & Social Studies |
|---|---|---|---|
| **1** — 300 headwords | • Eyes<br>• Fruit<br>• Trees<br>• Wheels | • At the Beach<br>• In the Sky<br>• Wild Cats<br>• Young Animals | • Art<br>• Schools |
| **2** — 450 headwords | • Electricity<br>• Plastic<br>• Sunny and Rainy<br>• Your Body | • Camouflage<br>• Earth<br>• Farms<br>• In the Mountains | • Cities<br>• Jobs |
| **3** — 600 headwords | • How We Make Products<br>• Sound and Music<br>• Super Structures<br>• Your Five Senses | • Amazing Minibeasts<br>• Animals in the Air<br>• Life in Rainforests<br>• Wonderful Water | • Festivals Around the World<br>• Free Time Around the World |
| **4** — 750 headwords | • All About Plants<br>• How to Stay Healthy<br>• Machines Then and Now<br>• Why We Recycle | • All About Desert Life<br>• All About Ocean Life<br>• Animals at Night<br>• Incredible Earth | • Animals in Art<br>• Wonders of the Past |
| **5** — 900 headwords | • Materials to Products<br>• Medicine Then and Now<br>• Transportation Then and Now<br>• Wild Weather | • All About Islands<br>• Animal Life Cycles<br>• Exploring Our World<br>• Great Migrations | • Homes Around the World<br>• Our World in Art |
| **6** — 1,050 headwords | • Cells and Microbes<br>• Clothes Then and Now<br>• Incredible Energy<br>• Your Amazing Body | • All About Space<br>• Caring for Our Planet<br>• Earth Then and Now<br>• Wonderful Ecosystems | • Food Around the World<br>• Helping Around the World |